THE WATKINS-FARNUM
PERFORMANCE SCALE

FORM A

A STANDARDIZED ACHIEVEMENT TEST FOR ALL BAND INSTRUMENTS

By
DR. JOHN G. WATKINS
AND
DR. STEPHEN E. FARNUM

TABLE OF CONTENTS

INTRODUCTION

To our knowledge, the Watkins-Farnum Performance Scale is the only standardized, objective testing method available for measuring performance and progress on a musical instrument.

Music teachers have long recognized the need for a reliable system of scoring student ability, and we believe this publication to be the answer.

Years of research and experimentation by Dr. Farnum have resulted in convincing proof of its reliability and validity, and also its usefulness in a variety of applications—for testing sight-reading ability, for band try-outs, for seating placement, or for testing annually or semi-annually to measure individual improvement.

Simple to administer, easy to grade with a minimum of paper work, the Watkins-Farnum Performance Scale promises to be an invaluable aid to the instrumental music instructor.

SUMMARY

A BRIEF SUMMARY OF THE CONSTRUCTION OF THE
WATKINS-FARNUM PERFORMANCE SCALE

The Watkins-Farnum Performance Scale for Band Instruments represents an adaptation of an original scale devised and standardized for the cornet.[1] This scale was carefully constructed to meet both musical and scientific criteria for reliability and validity. Briefly, the procedure for constructing the cornet scale was as follows:

The order in which the various symbols were introduced was determined from an analysis of twenty-three widely known teaching methods. These were selected from a large list of present-day American cornet methods according to the extent of their use as judged by a group of instrumental teachers throughout the country. A set of melodic exercises was written, ranging from the easiest type to one of professional grade. These melodies were constructed to measure sixteen separate levels of achievement. In them were introduced the various symbols of music notation, according to the order in which they are learned, as indicated by the preliminary study. The measure was designated as the unit of scoring. A standardized method for administering the test and marking errors was developed. Sixty-eight exercises were then administered to 105 cornet students of various levels of ability. The difficulty of playing each exercise with any given number of errors was computed. From the sixty-eight exercises two equivalent forms of fourteen each were selected. There was an equal increment of difficulty (mathematically determined) between each exercise. The two final forms of the test, called Form A and Form B, were equivalent in difficulty throughout their range. Based on scores made by the 105 cases in the preliminary testing, Form A and B correlated .982 with each other. The rank-order validity coefficients varied from .66 to .91, all except two being above .80. The internal consistency of both forms of the test was high, correlations between scores on the various exercises and scores on the entire test running between .44 and .93. Over half of these were above .80. The dispersions of scores on the respective exercises and on the entire test were approximately the same for both Forms A and B.

The final forms of the test were administered by music instructors to cornet students with varied abilities. The Sight Performance Score was obtained from a sight reading of the test. The Practiced Performance Score, or measure of technical skill, was obtained by administering the same test after the student had spent a week practicing it. Data was obtained on 153 students who took Form A. Seventy-one of these students also took Form B and a final reliability between the two forms amounted to .953 for Sight Reading and .947 for the Practiced Performance. Those interested in a more detailed description of the construction and validation procedures are referred to the published report of the original work.[1]

The Watkins-Farnum Performance Scale for Band Instruments is adapted from the Watkins Cornet Scale. In the Cornet Scale the difficult problem of procedure in constructing an objective measure of musical performance appears to have been mastered. One of its most noteworthy achievements is the grading of difficulty of the rhythm patterns. The rhythm patterns in the cornet scale are not confined to this particular instrument but apply as well to other instruments. With this in mind, the Watkins Cornet Performance Scale was adapted for all band instruments. The basic features of the cornet scale were kept and the following adaptations were made:

[1] John Watkins, "Objective Measurement of Instrumental Performance." New York, T. C. Bur. of Publications, Columbia University, 1942.

Watkins-Farnum Performance Scale Form A is based on material adapted from the John Watkins original Form B

SUMMARY (Cont.)

1. The scale was transposed into a key suitable for the instrument being tested.

2. The notes of the exercise were kept within the range of the instrument.

3. The limitations and difficulties of each instrument were not exceeded.

In order to find the reliability of the Watkins-Farnum Performance Scale, two forms of it were given to students in the instrumental music classes. These reliabilities are given in Table 1.

TABLE 1

RELIABILITY COEFFICIENTS FOR THE WATKINS-FARNUM
PERFORMANCE SCALE

CORRELATIONS BETWEEN FORM A AND B

Grade		Form A		Form B			
		M	σ	M	σ	r	σ meas.
7	32	30	6.3	30	6.3	.87	2.3
10-12	30	66	8.8	63	8.8	.94	2.2
7-12	75	51	10.4	51	9.8	.94	2.6

Watkins found in his study that the reliability coefficient between Form A and Form B was .95. He had 71 students in a wide age and grade range. The reliabilities in Table 1 were obtained when all the instruments in the band were used and compare favorably with those found by Watkins.

Validity

The validity of the Watkins-Farnum Performance Scale was found by using rank-order correlations. Students were first ranked by their instructors; each instructor placed his best student in number one position and the others in order of their ability. After this was done the students were tested on the Watkins-Farnum Performance Scale and received a score. A correlation was computed between the ranks given by the instructor and the score on the Scale, and are given in Table 2.

Table 2

CORRELATIONS BETWEEN SCORES ON THE WATKINS-FARNUM
PERFORMANCE SCALE AND TEACHER'S RANKINGS

Type of Musical Instrument	N	r
Clarinet and Saxophone (1)	26	.83
Drum	15	.68
Cornet and Trumpet	20	.87
Flute, Oboe, Bassoon	12	.86
Clarinet and Saxophone (2)	22	.85
Trombone, Baritone, Tuba	18	.78
Trumpet and French Horn	18	.77

Watkins' correlations on the cornet scale, based on 11 to 30 rankings, ranged from .69 to .90 with the majority being above .80. The correlations in Table 2 compare favorably with those of Watkins. In view of these high correlations the scale may be used with a high level of confidence in measuring achievement in instrumental music.

The teachers who ranked the students had worked with them for at least a year. Judgments were based on both technical ability and musicianly performance.

A more detailed report of the validation and reliability of the Watkins-Farnum Performance Scale is given in the thesis "The Prediction of Success in Instrumental Music" by Stephen E. Farnum. This thesis is in the library of the Harvard Graduate School of Education.

DIRECTIONS FOR THE ADMINISTRATION OF THE TEST
RULES FOR SCORING

The student starts with the first exercise. He should be stopped when he has made a zero score in two consecutive exercises.

The **measure** is the scoring unit and should be counted wrong if any error occurs within it. Score only **one error** in any one measure.

Subtract the number of wrong measures from the "possible" score indicated on the score sheet.

In order to indicate type of error made by the student, a code letter, written after each of the 8 types of errors, may be used. This would be written under the incorrect measure. If the code letter is not used then draw a cross through each measure played incorrectly.

INSTRUCTIONS TO STUDENT

A metronome should be used to indicate the correct tempo. The metronome should be turned off as soon as the student has started.

Use the following statement:

"IN THIS TEST YOU ARE TO READ EACH EXERCISE EXACTLY AS WRITTEN. BE SURE THAT YOU HOLD EACH NOTE IT'S CORRECT VALUE AND OBSERVE ALL MARKINGS AND SIGNS. THE GRADING WILL BE QUITE STRICT SO DO YOUR BEST. THE FIRST EXERCISE IS TO BE PLAYED AT THIS SPEED." Turn the metronome on at 88 beats per minute, the speed of the first exercise, and count one or two measures for the student. Then say, "START WHEN YOU ARE READY, I WILL TURN THE METRONOME OFF AFTER THE FIRST MEASURE." Run the metronome one measure and one beat into the second measure and then stop it.

UNDER NO CIRCUMSTANCES GIVE THE STUDENT HELP WHILE HE IS TAKING THE TEST, EXCEPT THAT AUTHORIZED IN THE SCORING RULES.

The student should pause no more than 15-20 seconds between exercises.

TYPES OF ERRORS

1. PITCH ERRORS (P)

    a. A tone added or a tone omitted constitutes an error.

    b. A tone played on the wrong pitch is an error.

        (1) Fuzzy attacks or minor irregularities in pitch during the course of an extended tone are not to be counted as errors, provided most of the note has been played on the right pitch.

        (2) If the student strikes the wrong pitch when attacking a note but correctly fingers it and **immediately** adjusts the lip to the correct pitch **without retonguing** the note, no error is to be counted. If he fingers it wrong, for example playing F sharp and then changing immediately to F natural, an error is counted.

DIRECTIONS FOR ADMINISTRATION (Cont.)

2. TIME ERRORS (R) for Rhythm

    a. Any note not given its correct value is marked wrong.

        (1) A sustained note must be held **within** one count of the correct beat. Thus, a whole note held for three full counts is marked wrong. If held for three counts and a little more it is considered right. It must extend over into the beginning of the fourth count. If it extends past the end of the fourth count, into the beginning of the fifth it again becomes wrong. Count to yourself and mark an error if the tone stops before you start to say the word "four" or after you have started to say the word "five".

        (2) Rule (1) above is to be applied to sustained tones, half notes, dotted halves, dotted quarters in six eight, etc. Be sure that the difference between the time any sustained tone is held and the correct time for it is less than a full beat.

3. CHANGE OF TIME ERRORS (T)

    a. If there is a marked increase or decrease in tempo, all measures played in the incorrect tempo are wrong.

        (1) If the increase or decrease in tempo within an exercise is less than twelve (12) beats per minute, no errors are to be marked. Before giving the tests, practice with the metronome to determine the limits and then use your judgment when administering the test.

        (2) Increase in Tempo.

            (a) Where the increase is in excess of twelve beats per minute, mark wrong only the measure in which the increase took place. If the increase has been gradual, mark the measure wrong in which you think it passed the twelve beats per minute mark of increase. (A return to normal tempo at any time is not counted as an error.)

        (3) Decrease in Tempo.

            (a) Where the decrease is in excess of twelve beats per minute, mark wrong all measures played at that retarded speed.

            (b) If the drop in speed is continued, mark four (4) measures wrong, and then, if the student seems wedded to the slower tempo, stop him and inform him that he is going too slow. Indicate the correct tempo with the metronome and let him start again at that point. If he again drops below the limit in tempo, say nothing but score all measures wrong which are played too slowly. (Follow the above procedure if the student fails to play exercise No. 9 in alla breve time.)

DIRECTIONS FOR ADMINISTRATION (Cont.)

4. EXPRESSION ERRORS (E)

    a. Failure to observe any expression mark constitutes an error.

        (1) The fact of the response, **not the degree** of the response, determines whether or not an error has been made.

            (a) Thus an increase in volume made when f follows p or mf indictaes that the student knows the meaning of Forte and has read the symbol correctly. The fact that he has increased volume too little or too much in the judgment of the scorer shall not be counted as an error. Be convinced only that the student has seen the mark, knows what it means, and indicates so by responding to it.

        (2) Failure to observe a crescendo, decrescendo, accelerando, or ritardo constitutes a single error which is ascribed to the measure in which the sign originates.

5. SLUR ERRORS (S)

    a. A slur omitted, a tongued note slurred, a slur carried onto notes which should be tongued, or a broken slur are all counted as errors.

        (1) Occasionally one finds a student who has been taught to play with an especially legato tongue. Do not mark slur errors when you first discover this, but inform him it is his responsibility to distinguish between slurred and tongued notes. After that, grade him as strictly as others. If in doubt, mark an error. The burden of proof lies with the student. See that he understands that and then score rigidly.

6. RESTS (R) as this will also be a rhythm error

    a. Ignoring a rest or failure to give a rest its correct value is an error. Apply same standards as to a sustained note. (see Rule 2)

7. HOLDS AND PAUSES (R) Rhythm error

    a. Holds written thus $\frown$ should be treated in the same way as other expression marks. (See section 4a, rule (1))

    b. **Pauses between measures,** no matter how long, are not to be counted as errors; however, do not inform the student of this fact.

    c. **Pauses between notes within the measure** are to be counted as errors.

8. REPEATS :‖

    a. Record an error if the pupil fails to make the repeat in No. 4 but score only the first rendition. In No. 7, score only the first rendition plus the second ending. Allow the student to complete the repeat but do not change the scoring or mark any new errors until the second ending.

        (1) If he should stop and ask you **immediately** whether he should repeat, answer, "Of course, play it exactly as written" and do not record an error. Failure to play the second ending on the repeat in No. 7 constitutes an error on the first measure of the second ending. In this case, tell the student to start on the second ending and finish.

SPECIAL INSTRUCTIONS
PROGRESS CHART

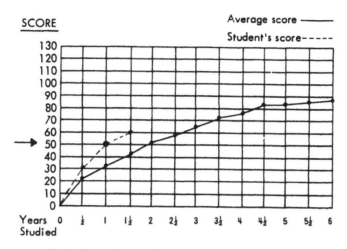

The progress chart above (reproduced on each score sheet) represents a general average score over a period of six years of study, and is a valuable means of recording and comparing the progress of your students. As an example, we have marked the chart for a student who had a score of 30 on the scale after ½ year of study, 50 after a year of study, and 60 after a year and a half. By using a broken line it is simple to compare his progress with that of the average made by all students in the school. This student's score would be considerably above average.

The chart is based on thousands of scores from the schools in one city, and in this city the beginning instrumental classes are started in the seventh grade. It would be desirable for schools to compile their own figures and to make up charts which would reflect experiences and teachings in that particular city.

When grades and scores are received from users of this scale new charts and norms will be derived.

GRADES

Group 1

Cornet	Flute
Clarinet (Sop.)	Saxophone
Alto Clarinet	Baritone
Bass Clarinet	

Group 2

Trombone	Oboe
Tuba	Bassoon
French Horn	Drum

GRADES FOR GROUP 1 INSTRUMENTS												
Years	½	1	1½	2	2½	3	3½	4	4½	5	5½	6
A	35	50	62	70	77	83	88	90	92	94	96	98
B	25	40	48	55	61	66	70	74	78	82	84	86
C	15	30	35	40	45	50	54	58	62	65	67	69
D	5	15	25	30	35	40	44	47	50	52	54	56

GRADES FOR GROUP 2 INSTRUMENTS												
Years	½	1	1½	2	2½	3	3½	4	4½	5	5½	6
A	25	40	52	60	67	73	78	80	84	88	90	92
B	15	30	38	45	51	56	60	64	68	72	74	76
C	5	15	25	30	35	40	44	48	52	55	57	59
D	0	5	15	20	25	30	34	37	40	42	44	46

Sample – Clarinet score is 68 at 4 years, grade – C
Trombone score is 50 at 2 years, grade – B

(Each score is the minimum in each grade classification)

The grading chart above (also reproduced on each score sheet) was designed as a suggested approach for simplifying the determination of letter grades. For example, if a clarinet score is 68 with four years of study, his grade is C, if a trombone scores 50 with two years of study his grade is B. By averaging the scores of a hundred trombones, after a year of study it was found that their scores were 10 points lower than were the scores for a 100 clarinets after a year of study. It was found that by rough grouping the instruments could be divided into 2 groups. The data on which these charts are based may be obtained from Dr. Stephen Farnum. He would also appreciate receiving scores in order to compile regional and national norms.

WATKINS-FARNUM PERFORMANCE SCALE EXERCISES

Bb Cornet, Baritone

B ♭ Cornet, Baritone 𝄞

B♭ Cornet, Baritone

B♭ Cornet, Baritone 𝄞

Bb Cornet, Baritone 𝄞

WATKINS-FARNUM PERFORMANCE SCALE EXERCISES

Soprano Clarinet, Alto Clarinet, Bass Clarinet*

*When written in octaves, Soprano Clarinets play upper notes, Alto and Bass Clarinets play lower notes.

Soprano Clarinet, Alto Clarinet, Bass Clarinet

Soprano Clarinet, Alto Clarinet, Bass Clarinet

Soprano Clarinet, Alto Clarinet, Bass Clarinet

Soprano Clarinet, Alto Clarinet, Bass Clarinet

WATKINS-FARNUM PERFORMANCE SCALE EXERCISES

Saxophone, Oboe*

*When written in octaves, Saxophones play upper notes, Oboe play lower notes.

Saxophone, Oboe

Saxophone, Oboe

Saxophone, Oboe

Saxophone, Oboe

WATKINS-FARNUM PERFORMANCE SCALE EXERCISES

Flute

Flute

Flute

Flute

Flute

WATKINS-FARNUM PERFORMANCE SCALE EXERCISES
French Horn

French Horn

French Horn

French Horn

French Horn

Trombone, Baritone 𝄢, Bassoon

Trombone, Baritone 𝄢, Bassoon

Trombone, Baritone 𝄢, Bassoon

Trombone, Baritone 𝄢, Bassoon

Trombone, Baritone 𝄢, Bassoon

WATKINS-FARNUM PERFORMANCE SCALE EXERCISES

Tuba

Tuba

Tuba

Tuba

Tuba

Snare Drum*

*The Snare Drum test consists of 12 exercises only.

Snare Drum

Snare Drum

Snare Drum